YIDDISH

DICK AND JANE

YIDDISH

WITH

DICK AND JANE

Ellis Weiner
Barbara Davilman

Illustrations by Gabi Payn

Little, Brown and Company
New York   Boston

Copyright © 2004 by Ellis Weiner and Barbara Davilman
Illustrations copyright © 2004 by Gabi Payn

Dick and Jane® is a registered trademark of Pearson Education, Inc.

Little, Brown and Company
Time Warner Book Group
1271 Avenue of the Americas, New York, NY 10020
Visit our Web site at www.twbookmark.com

First Edition

Library of Congress Cataloging-in-Publication Data
Weiner, Ellis.
    Yiddish with Dick and Jane / Ellis Weiner and Barbara Davilman; illustrations by Gabi Payn. — 1st ed.
        p. cm.
    ISBN 0-316-15972-7
    1. Readers (Primary) — Humor. 2. Yiddish language — Humor. 3. Elson, William H. (William Harris), 1856 – 1935 — Parodies, imitations, etc. 4. Gray, William S. (William Scott), 1885 – 1960 — Parodies, imitations, etc. I. Davilman, Barbara. II. Payn, Gabi. III. Title.

PN6231.R36W45 2004
439'.186421'0207 — dc22   2004006753

10 9 8 7 6 5 4

LAKE
Book Design by Meryl Sussman Levavi
Printed in the United States of America

YIDDISH

WITH

DICK AND JANE

See Jane.

Jane is married to Bob.

Jane loves Bob very much.

Bob is a real *mensch*.

Jane and Bob have two children.
Their names are Katie and Scott.
They do well in school and help
take care of Max and Whiskers.

"What good kids we have,"
say Jane and Bob.
"*Kina-hora.*"

Jane shows Bob and the kids the pretty purse she bought for Ellen's birthday.

Ellen is Jane's best friend.

"I wanted to get something nice for Ellen," says Jane.
"I did not want to get a piece of *schlock*."

Jane works in real estate.

Today is Sunday.

Jane has an Open House.

She must *schlep* the Open House
signs to the car.

See Jane *schlep*.

Schlep, Jane. *Schlep*.

Schlep, schlep, schlep.

Bob takes Katie and Scott to visit
Jane's mother.
Katie and Scott visit Grandmother
a lot.
She has been feeling *ibbledick* lately.

See Stanley.

He is Jane's boss.

He comes to the Open House.

He puts fresh flowers and scented
candles everywhere.

He is a *shtikl* artistic and
just has that gift.

Jane likes Open Houses.

She likes meeting new people.

She even likes the *shnorrers* who come just to *nosh*.

Nosh, shnorrers, nosh.
Nosh, nosh, nosh.

Bob and Katie and Scott arrive
at Grandmother's house.
They ring the bell and
wait for *Bubbe* to open
the door.

Gornisht.

They ring again.

And again.

And again.

Takeh gornisht.

Bob finds the spare key
under the mat.
He opens the door.

"Oy gevalt!"

Jane goes to see Ellen.
Jane gives Ellen her birthday
present.

"*Mazel tov*, Ellen!" says Jane.

"What a beautiful purse!" says Ellen.
"I cannot accept this, Jane."

"*Es gezunterheyt*, Ellen," insists
Jane.

Ellen brings out coffee and
Entenmann's.
They nibble and *kibbitz* for a while.

Bob and Katie and Scott sit by
Grandmother.
They wait for the ambulance.

"Father," asks Katie, "will *Bubbe*
be okay?"

"Of course, Katie," says Bob.
"She is just a little *tsedoodelt*."

They hear the siren outside.

The paramedics *tanz*
themselves in.

The paramedics examine
Grandmother.

"*Nu?*" asks Bob.

The paramedics put Grandmother
onto a stretcher.

One paramedic looks at Bob.

"*Nisht geferlich,*" says the
paramedic.

The paramedics carry Grandmother
to the ambulance.
They drive her to the hospital.

Bob takes out his cell phone to call
Jane.
"When your mother hears this she
will *plotz*," says Bob.

Bob tells Jane the news.

"Your mother is not in pain, Jane," says Bob.
"But she is slightly *tsedreyt in kop*."

See Dick.
Dick is Jane's brother.

Dick is playing golf with Tom.
He borrows Tom's sand wedge.

Tom is Dick's oldest
chaver.

Tom and Dick play golf with Frank and Steve.

Dick wants Frank and Steve's business.

Dick *schmoozes* with them.

See Dick *schmooze*.

Schmooze, Dick. *Schmooze*.

Schmooze, schmooze, schmooze.

Dick gets a call on
his cell phone.
It is Jane.

"I am *schmoozing* on the golf
course, Jane," says Dick.
"Can I call you back?"

"No, Dick," says Jane. "We have
tsuris."
Jane tells Dick what has happened.

"*Oy vey*, Jane," says Dick.

Jane also leaves a message for
her sister, Sally.
Sally teaches a course in
Transgressive Feminist Ceramics.
She lives in Berkeley.
She might as well be in *Hotzeplotz*.

Dick drives to the hospital.

He stops for a red light.

He sees Tom's wife, Susan, coming
out of a Courtyard by Marriott.

She is wearing a dress up to her
pupik.

Susan is with Dick's friend Phil.
Phil puts his arm around Susan.

"I wonder why they are at that
motel," thinks Dick.
"They must be going to a party to
celebrate some *simcha*."

Jane and Bob and Katie and Scott
wait to hear from the doctor.
They read old copies of *McCall's*
and sit on *shpilkes*.

Old people *shmy* up and down
the hallways.
They *shmy* and talk to themselves.

"Why do they do that, Father?" asks
Katie. "Are they *meshugge*?"

"The lady with the housecoat on her
head is *meshugge*, Katie," says Bob.
"But the man hitting himself in the
chest with the spoon is *farmisht*."

Dick arrives.

"Jane, Bob, Katie, and Scott, how is Mother?" asks Dick.

"We are still waiting for the doctor," says Bob.

"I am getting a little *nudjedik*, Dick," says Jane.

See Doctor Patrick O'Shaughnessy.
He is a cardiologist and a *sheygets*.

"Hello, Dick and Jane," says Doctor
O'Shaughnessy.
"I will give you the *emess*.

"Your mother has had a small stroke.
She will be a little
lethargic and
sporadically
farblondget.
She will need
full-time care."

See Priscilla.

Dick and Jane have hired Priscilla
to take care of Mother.
Priscilla is from the island of
Jamaica.
She is a real *hilf*.

Sally calls Jane.

"I got your message, Jane," says
Sally.
"I am on my way."

"Oh, Sally, don't make a *tsimmes*,"
says Jane.
"Mother is fine.
You do not have to come."

"Do not tell me what to do, Jane,"
says Sally.

See Betty.

Jane runs into Betty at the
supermarket.

Betty's husband left her for another
woman.

Betty is not a close friend.

But Jane has *rachmones* for her.

Betty is in a good mood.
She has a new job.
She reaches into her purse.

"Look at my *fancy-schmancy* new card, Jane," says Betty.

Jane sees Betty's purse.
It is the same purse Jane gave Ellen for her birthday!

"Ellen must have given my gift to Betty," thinks Jane.
"Ellen must not have liked it."

Jane feels *nisht gut*.

"What is wrong, Jane?" asks Betty. "You look a little *farshadat*."

"I just remembered I have *latkes* in the oven, Betty," lies Jane. "I have to go."

Jane runs out of the market.

Dick has a business dinner with
Frank and Steve.
Frank and Steve are running late.

Dick waits at the *heymish* bar.
The lights in the bar are low.

See Susan and Phil!

Susan and Phil are in a booth.

Susan and Phil are drinking margaritas.

Susan and Phil are holding hands.

"I did not know Phil drank margaritas," thinks Dick.

"And he is having it with salt, *noch*."

Jane gets home.

"I can't believe what a *shtunk* Ellen turned out to be, Bob," says Jane.

Jane tells Bob about Betty and the purse.

"Now, now, Jane," says Bob.
"Don't make such a *shtuss*.
There must be some explanation."

Just then, the doorbell rings.
Bob gets up off his *tuchas* and answers the door.

See Sally!

"Sally!" says Bob.
"What a nice surprise."

"*Vo den*, Bob?" says Sally.
"I told Jane I was coming.
Don't the two of you speak?"

Sally comes into the house.

"Hello, Sally," says Jane.
"You look wonderful.
That is a nice outfit."

"No it isn't," says Sally.
"This is a *schmatte*."

Sally tells Jane that she wants to see Mother.

"She is asleep now, Sally," says Jane.
"By eight o'clock Mother is completely *oysgeshpilt*.
Come with us to meet Dick and his family for dinner," says Jane.

"Are we going to Pagoda Dragon, Jane?" asks Sally.

"No, Sally," says Jane.
"We are meeting them at Golden Noodle Pavilion.
Pagoda Dragon is *mechuleh*."

Jane, Bob, Sally, Katie, and Scott
drive to the restaurant.

"Is something wrong, Jane?" says
Sally. "You are all *fartootst.*"

"Jane is upset because she gave her
friend Ellen a nice purse," says Bob.
"And Ellen gave the purse to Betty."

"Are you sure it is the same one?"
asks Sally.

"Yes," says Jane.
"The man said it is one of a kind.
He is the purse *maven*."

"You should tell Ellen that it makes
you mad that she gave your gift
away, Jane," says Sally.

"It does not make me mad, Sally," says Jane.

"Well, it should," says Sally.

See Mary.
Mary is Dick's wife.

See Dick and Mary's children.
Their names are Alice and Zach.

Everyone is at the Chinese restaurant.
Alice and Zach are eating the crunchy noodles in the bowl.

"Stop *fressing* those noodles, Alice and Zach," says Mary.
"It will spoil your dinner."

Jane, Sally, Bob, Katie, and Scott get to the restaurant.

"Jane," whispers Sally. "I thought Susan was married to Tom."

"Susan *is* married to Tom, Sally," says Jane.

"Then who is that *schmo*?" asks Sally.

"That is Phil," says Jane.

"I thought Phil was married to Bev,"
says Sally.

"Phil *is* married to Bev," says Jane.

"*Hoo-hah!*" thinks Sally.

Jane, Bob, Sally, Katie, and Scott get
to the table.
Everyone says hello and gets settled.

"I love their Lake Tung Ting Shrimp,"
says Bob.

"Do you like shrimp, Aunt Sally?"
asks Zach.

"Shrimp?" says Sally. *"Feh!"*

"Look, Dick," says Sally.
"Tom's wife, Susan, is kissing Phil."

"Yes, Sally, they are good friends,"
says Dick.

"That is not how friends kiss, Dick,"
says Sally.
"I think Susan and Phil are
shtupping."

"Oh no," says Dick.
"They are just happy to see each
other."

"Susan is such a *bren*," says Jane.

"Come on, Dick and Jane," says Sally. "This is a *shanda*."

"What is?" asks Dick.

"Oh, never mind," says Sally. "Pass the *Mu Shoo*."

The next night, Bob and Jane and
Sally go to Ellen's birthday dinner.

Ellen shows off the beautiful purse
that Jane gave her.

Jane is very confused.

"Look, Bob and Sally," says Jane.
"Ellen did not give my purse to
Betty! Betty must have bought
her own purse.
I feel like such a *shmegegge*."

"You are not a *shmegegge*, Jane,"
says Sally.
"The man who sold you the purse
lied. He said it was one of a kind.
But it was not. He is a *goniff*!
Someone ought to give him a *zetz* in
the *schnoz*."

The next day Dick picks up Jane and Sally.
They drive to visit Mother.
They drive near Tom's house.

"I should stop and give Tom his sand wedge back," says Dick.
"He has been *hokking me a tshynik* about it all week."

Dick parks the car in front of Tom's house.

Someone comes out of Tom's house.
It is Stanley!

"What is Stanley doing there?" asks
Dick.

"Maybe Tom wants Stanley to sell
the house for him," says Jane.
"You know how Tom hates to
handl."

Tom comes out.
Tom kisses Stanley on the mouth.

Sally starts to laugh.

"No wonder Susan is with Phil," says
Sally. "Tom is gay!"

"Tom is more than gay, Sally," says Dick. "He is overjoyed."

"Of course," says Jane.
"Stanley must have just told Tom what a good price he can get on his house."

"*Oy Gotenyu*," sighs Sally.

Dick and Jane and Sally go to
Mother's house.
Mother *kvells* when she sees Sally.

"Sally!" says Mother.
"You look wonderful.
You have not changed a bit."

"Yes I have, Mother," says Sally.
"I am fat and I have a mustache.
I am a big *meeskite*."

"You are not fat, Sally," says Mother.
"You are *zaftig*."

"Mother," says Sally.
"Look at me."

"I am looking at you, Sally," says
Mother.
"You look just like you used to."

Mother holds up a picture.

It is a picture of Dick and Jane and
Sally.
In the picture they are children.
Mother and Father and Spot and
Puff are also in the picture.

"See?" says Mother.

"Everyone is so *freylech.*"

Sally points to the picture.

"I am not like this anymore, Mother.
The world is not like this.
People are not nice.
They are mean.
I am on MatchMeIfYouCan.com and
every man I meet is a *shlemiel*.

"I am lonely, frustrated, bored, and
overweight.
My boss is a *putz* and I hate my
hair."

"Your hair is beautiful, Sally," says
Mother.

"You did not help me to get ready to
live in the real world!" cries Sally.

"I raised you to live in the world that
I lived in, dear," says Mother.

Sally gives up.
She goes downstairs.

Priscilla is dusting in the living
room.
She is smoking a big cigarette that
she rolled herself.

"Did you have a nice visit with your ma?" asks Priscilla.

"It made me sad," says Sally.

"Why are you sad?" asks Priscilla.
"Your ma is happy.
Your brother Dick and sister Jane
are happy, too.
The whole *mishpocha* is happy."

"Mother and Dick and Jane *are* happy," says Sally.
"But I am not.
I live in the real world.
Mother and Father did not teach me how to live in the real world.
I do not know how to deal with all of its *mishegas*."

Priscilla hands Sally the cigarette.
"Take a toke of the spliff and you be all right," says Priscilla.

Sally takes a toke of the spliff.
It is a *mechayeh*.

"We always being raised to live our
parents' life," says Priscilla.
"And their parents raised them
the same way.
That's why we got to go out into
the world and unlearn it all.
You think my ma taught me to come
to the U.S. to work for some white
alter kocker?"

Sally thinks that Priscilla is very wise.

"I have to ask you a question,
Priscilla," says Sally.
"Do you have any *rugalach*?"

The next day Dick and Jane take Sally to the airport so she can fly back to Berkeley.

"We are so glad you visited, Sally," says Jane.

"I am glad, too, Jane," says Sally. Sally kisses Dick and Jane good-bye.

"Thank you for taking good care of Mother," says Sally.
"And thank you for hiring Priscilla. She is a real *chachem*."

Sally goes through Security.

Dick and Jane watch as Sally
empties the *dreck* from her purse.
It goes through the X-ray machine.

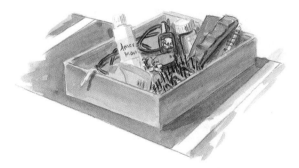

Sally waves and walks off toward
her plane.

"I have an idea, Dick!" cries Jane. "Someday soon, let's all go visit Sally in Berkeley.
We will bring Katie and Scott and Alice and Zach and we will not tell Sally we are coming."

"That is a fine idea, Jane," says Dick. "Won't Sally be surprised!"

(But that is a whole different *megillah*.)

The End

Authors' Note

Why, people have asked, drag Dick and Jane into a book about Yiddish?

Our answer is: We haven't. We've dragged Yiddish into a book about Dick and Jane — and about the sunny pastoral world they share with friendly milkmen, doctors who make house calls, mommies who wear dresses, and daddies who look no older than eighteen.

Yiddish with Dick and Jane is a parody novelette on a series of important themes: what happens when the idealized universe of our favorite childhood characters collides with modern-day reality, the inevitable limitations of parenting, the sharp contrast between successive generations' outlooks, and the damage that can result from dealing with a dishonest handbag salesman.

Sally, for once, is the book's heroine, news of which we know will be received with joy by Sally fans the world over. And her story has nothing to do with learning Yiddish. Rather, it concerns her discovery that the blessings of a perfect childhood can be deceiving, and often have to be paid for later in life.

We use the Yiddish like a series of flares, little bursts of irony, worldliness, and savvy to illuminate the dopey innocence of Dick and Jane's world. It's a world in which Sally once lived and which we, as children, once visited and took at face value.

Of course we're all sophisticated adults now, and impervious to the allure of its cheery, oblivious simplicities. We know better.

But how much better might we know better if our primers had included *mishegas* and *mensch?*

— E.W.

Yeah. What he said.

— B.D.

Glossary of
Yiddish Words

Many of the words defined here have multiple meanings, most of which we ignore. Instead, the entry explains the word's usage in the text. (This is Yiddish with Dick and Jane, *not* Yiddish with James Joyce.*) Sources include Leo Rosten's* The Joys of Yiddish, *some deli's kooky website, our own personal experience, and our mothers. Faith Jones, at the New York Public Library, helped us sort out conflicting viewpoints.*

Note that the letter combination ch *calls for a guttural rasp in the back of the throat, as in the Scottish word* loch *or the universally (more or less) known toast* L'chaim.

alter kocker (OLL-ter KAH-ker) – Literally, "old shitter." A grumpy, cranky, cantankerous old man. A bit more caustic than "old fart." Can also refer to a woman or a mixed group, e.g., "No way I'm going to the matinee. All the *alter kockers* will still be divvying up the lunch check halfway through the first act." Often used in its abbreviated form, *A.K.*

bren (bren) – A person of great vitality, charisma, and energy. From the verb *brennen*, "to burn." Mnemonic hint: A good way to remember that *brennen* means "to burn" is to recall Walter Brennan, that fiery, smoldering, burning movie and TV actor who played fiery, smoldering Grandpa on *The Real McCoys*.

bubbe (BUB-eh or BUB-bee or BOOH-beh or BOOH-bee) – Grandmother. Rhymes with . . . well, with something that sounds similar. Its diminutive, *boobeleh*, is a term of endearment or affection between spouses, of parents toward their children, or between showbiz people who are either being heavily ironic or are unaware of the fact that no one has used it in this way with a straight face since 1954.

chachem (CHAW-chem) – A wise person (man or woman), a sage. To the question "How can you know a person is wise unless you yourself are wise enough to recognize their wisdom?" we say, Don't ask.

chaver (CHAH-ver) – A guy's best pal. Friend, chum.

dreck (drek) – Literally, excrement or dung. Something——merchandise, a work of art, etc.—— that's cheap, lousy, meretricious junk (i.e., even worse than *schlock*). "We saw their new house. Believe me, the furnishings are strictly from Dreck Barn."

emess (EH-mess) – The real, unvarnished, unmitigated truth, with claims to objectivity or universal validity, e.g., "You want the *emess?* They'll never get divorced. They hate each other too much."

es gezunterheyt (ESS geh-ZOONT-er-HATE) – Literally, "Eat in good health," meaning, Enjoy!

fancy-schmancy (fancy-SHMAN-see) – Pretentiously fancy, although when Betty says it she's mocking, lightly, her own potential pretentiousness. The addition of *schm-* to the beginning of a word is also a popular way to minimize the subject as being relatively trivial or otherwise dismissable, compared to what you're about to say. E.g., "Emmy schmemmy, the show stinks."

farblondget (far-BLUN-jet) – Lost, confused, wandering around, wildly astray. "I go to Starbucks for a lousy cup of coffee, I take one look at the grande this and vente that, with the macchiato and the caramel latte cream, I get totally *farblondjet*."

farmisht (far-MISHT)–Not "famished," which isn't even Yiddish (although, since it means "really, really hungry," it could be a sort of honorary Yiddish), but rather, confused, addled, dysfunctional.

farshadat (far-SHAH-det)–Pained, wounded. One of us (E.W.) heard Cindy Lauper use this in an interview!

fartootst (far-TOOTS'T, rhymes with "car foots'd," although also can be said "fah-TOOTS'T")–Disoriented, confused, distracted. In this case, Jane is more the latter—more *fartootst* than *oysgeshpilt*.

feh (feh)–Expression of distaste or disgust. We know someone who, when asked if he had dogs or cats as pets when he was growing up, replied, "Never. My mother used to say, 'Animals in the house? *Feh!*'"

fressing (FRESS-ing)–A Yiddish word *(fress)* with an English suffix. *Fress* means to eat heartily, to eat a lot, to eat indelicately or wolf one's food. You *nosh* for fun and recreation and to be sociable. You *ess* when you're hungry. You *fress* because you're a big fat pig.

freylech (FRY-lich)–Happy, cheerful, upbeat. Used more to describe a general personality trait than a specific response—and usually concerns the behavior of others rather than one's own mood. "Prozac schmozac, at least she's more *freylech* now (*kinahora*)."

goniff (GAHN-iff)–A thief, a crook. Older generations have also used it admiringly, to mean rascal, but its main usage has narrowed down to something plainly derogatory. For this reason one hardly ever hears Robin Hood referred to anymore as "that *goniff.*"

gornisht (GORE-nisht)–Nothing, nada, zip, zilch—and in a bad way. Not "What do you want on your hamburger, Sol?" "*Gornisht.*" But rather, "What do you want on your hamburger, Sol?" "What do I want on my hamburger? I'll tell you what I want on my hamburger. I want your sister should give me a little respect when she calls and I answer the phone. Instead I say hello and she right away asks for you. I get *gornisht.* That's what I want on my hamburger."

handl (HAHN-dl)–Literally, "to be in business." To bargain, deal, negotiate. Often said with accompanying hand gestures signaling juggling, balancing, weighing one thing against another. *Antonym:* Paying retail.

heymish (HAME-ish)–Homey (as an adjective, not a noun). Can be used about people as well as about places: "The Archbishop of Canterbury? Lovely man. Very *heymish*, for an Anglican."

hilf (hilf)–A real help, a godsend.

hokking me a tshynik (HOCK-ing me a CHYE-nik)–Literally, "banging me a teakettle." Relentlessly talking or jabbering—but really, nagging or badgering about something to the point of abuse or unreasonableness. *Hok*, used alone, can be a bit milder, and can mean urge, exhort, pitch, ask. "It's Pledge Week on NPR. Every station you tune in, they're *hokking* you to be a member."

hoo-hah (HOO-HAH, with both syllables accented)– "Do tell!" "You don't say!" "Hubba hubba!" "Hoo boy!" An expression denoting excited or titillated interest. "Guess who's going to be at the seder! Beyonce!" *"Hoo-hah!"*

Hotzeplotz (HOTS-a-plots) – Timbuktu, the middle of nowhere. Used not by the mover but by the person who is moved away from. Suggests an unfathomable distance or an unreasonably (and, really, hurtfully) obscure place. "Visit? How can I visit when you live on the moon now?" "Ma, I'm ten miles away." "Honey, it might as well be *Hotzeplotz*."

ibbledick (IB-bl-dick) – Literally, "nauseated," "barfy." Vaguely unwell, out of sorts. N.B.: There is no Yiddish phrase for feeling "in sorts." Then again, there is no English phrase for it either, so never mind.

kibbitz (KIB-bits) – To chat, gab, engage in frivolous conversation. Once commonly used in connection with card games, for someone who hangs out but doesn't play. "I'm broke. You guys play. I'll *kibbitz*." Not to be confused with *kibbutz* (kih-BUUTZ, rhyming with "rib toots," as in "tootsie"), which is a communal farm. The one thing you don't have a chance to do on a *kibbutz* is *kibbitz*.

kina-hora (KINE-a-HOAR-a or, more colloquially, KIN-na-HOAR-a) – Reflexive magical phrase to ward off the evil eye (similar to "knock wood"). E.g., "It doesn't look like my son will be indicted, *kina-hora.*"

kvell (kvel—i.e., one syllable)–To beam with pride and joy, usually parental or grandparental. The accepted and in fact inevitable response when someone *kvells* at you is to squirm and become self-conscious and generally act like an embarrassed twelve-year-old—which, to the *kveller*, you essentially still are.

latkes (LOT-kiss)–Potato pancakes. It's possible that Betty knows that Jane is lying, because you don't bake *latkes* in the oven. You cook them in oil in a skillet. It makes you wonder: Does Betty know how to make *latkes*?

maven (MAY-ven)–An expert, an authority—either really or derisively. Real: "Ask Tom. He's the electron microscope maven." Derisive: "Put that slide down! Who do you think you are, the electron microscope maven?"

mazel tov (MAH-zl tuv)–Literally, "good luck" (*mazel* means luck, as in, "Talk about *mazel*—he got out one day before the stock went south"). Used colloquially to mean congratulations, but is often reserved to convey moral approval of the thing being celebrated, to suggest that the celebration is particularly deserved: a birth to people you like, the marriage of nice people (or of the children of nice people), an award won for real merit. To an obscure Tasmanian novelist for winning the Nobel Prize: "Congratulations." To Philip Roth: *"Mazel tov!"*

mechayeh (meh-CHAI-eh) – A pleasure, a delight, combining the physical and the emotional. "Cancún? Please. The beach was a hundred degrees. Like an *oven*. Any little breeze was a *mechayeh*."

mechuleh (meh-CHOO-leh, with the guttural *ch*) – Bankrupt, kaput—a business, a marriage, whatever. See how the letters for "kaput" are in the word "bankrupt"? Isn't language great?

meeskite (MEESE-kite) – An ugly person or thing—even a sentiment. Most often used with regard to women. But then, Judaism is the religion where the Orthodox men have a prayer thanking God they weren't born women, so there you are.

megillah (meh-GIL-lah) – The Megillah is the Book of Esther, a long, tedious account read in synagogue during the holiday of Purim. Thus, a lengthy story or recitation of events full of boring detail: "Then somebody asked him about his prostate operation, and we had to sit through the whole *megillah.*"

mensch (mench) – Literally, "person." Here, a mature, admirable, unselfish human being. "That editorial made me so upset. But Timmy got up from his video game and went all the way to the bathroom to bring me the Xanax, the little *mensch.*"

meshugge (meh-SHOOH-geh, rhymes with "boogie-woogeh") – Crazy, wacky—but used lovingly. "I can't meet you for lunch. I'm waiting for my *meshugge* plumber to *tanz* himself over here and fix the drip in my bathroom."

mishegas (mish-eh-GOSS, says Rosten, but we've also heard MISH-eh-goss) – An absurd or ridiculous idea or belief; irrational behavior; individual, eccentric craziness, which encompasses everything from minor tics to major neuroses, but not outright psychosis. "Forget dinner at your mother's. I can't deal with her running around in her bra and all her other *mishegas.*"

mishpocha (mish-PUH-chuh) – The whole family. Not necessarily the entire extended family, from all over the place plus Israel, but everyone within a reasonable distance. Can be used metaphorically: "We had a working lunch at the Italian place— everybody in Sales, the whole *mishpocha.*"

Mu Shoo (MOO SHOO, with both syllables accentuated)–A popular Chinese dish, consisting of shredded vegetables and meat wrapped in a thin flour pancake spread with hoisin sauce, and, as such, a sort of honorary Yiddish term. ("Really?" No. Not really.)

nisht geferlich (NISHT geh-FAIR-lich)–"I've seen worse." Manages to compress good news and bad news into a single phrase—which, in Yiddish, a language of tragic-but-ironic acceptance, amounts to a cry of joy.

nisht gut (nisht GUT)–Literally, "no good." Used to mean no good, as in "bad." Sorry. But sometimes a word just means what it means.

noch (nooch or noch, rhyming with "cook" or "lock," with the guttural *ch* sound)–In addition, even, moreover, yet—but more fun, more ironic, and much punchier. "He got out of prison—and ran for Congress! And won, *noch.*"

nosh (nahsh)–As a verb, to eat in bites, to graze or

snack. More polite nibbling than actual eating. However, as a noun—i.e., if you invite people over for a *nosh*—it means you serve just as much food, if not more, than the Fountainbleu does for its buffet brunch.

Nu? (new)–"Well?" "So?" "What's new?" "What's happening?" "Any news?" Also, ironically: "What did you expect?" "And you're surprised?" It's not really spelled with a question mark, but if you leave it out people will think you mean the thirteenth letter of the Greek alphabet. And no one wants that.

nudjedik (NOODGE-eh-dik)–Anxious, antsy. Your daughter takes the train back to *Hotzeplotz*. It's supposed to arrive at 11:30. You check. It does. It's now almost 1 a.m. and you still haven't heard that she made it home. You start to get *nudjedik*.

oy gevalt (OY geh-VULT, or OY geh-VAHLT)–"Oh no!" "Woe is me." Expression of dismay that vaguely suggests unhappy or worrisome ramifications. "She's dating a Republican? *Oy gevalt!*"

oy Gotenyu (oy GAWT-ten-yu)–*Oy* is the universal exclamation, of the family that includes the English "Oh!" and the Spanish "Ai!" *Gotenyu* invokes *Got*

(God), as in "God help us." "She ordered corned beef on whole wheat? *Oy Gotenyu!*"

oysgeshpilt (OYS-geh-shpilt, where the first syllable rhymes with "Royce.")–Worn out. Also passé, something that's run its course. A terrific Scrabble word, if Yiddish were allowed, which it isn't.

oy vey (OY VAY, with both syllables emphasized)– "Oh no," "Oh my God," etc.—e.g., what a person says when the TiVo breaks down right before the season premiere of *The Sopranos*. It's an involuntary response to the unexpected, like a sneeze. "The elevator's *broken*? They live seven flights up!" (Sigh.) "*Oy vey.*"

plotz (plahts)–Literally, "to explode." To fall over from bad news or to burst from good news. Can go either way. But this is how one reacts to feelings: by exploding or fainting. Nothing in between.

pupik (PUH-pik, the *u* rhyming with *oo* in "hook")– Technically, "bellybutton." Professionally, used by mothers describing the length of the skirt on the *shiksa* (see *sheygets*) that their only son brings home. "In walks this 'Bridgette,' with the blonde hair, probably bleached, in a dress up to her *pupik*."

putz (putts, rhyming with "huts")–A fool, a ninny, a simpleminded jerk. Also slang for penis.

rachmones (rahch-MUN-ness)–Compassion, fellow feeling, empathy, pity. "The Rachmones" would also make a very nice name for a sensitive Yiddish punk rock group.

rugalach (ROOG-eh-lach)–German pastry consisting of small, rolled-up flaky minicrescents baked with nuts, raisins, chocolate, cinnamon, etc. Crumbly, dense, and chewy. Great with coffee. No matter how often you put them out intending them to be a *nosh*, you always end up *fressing* them.

schlep (shlep)–To lug or carry laboriously; to travel arduously or simply over an unnecessarily long distance, e.g., "Of course I invited Magellan! But he can't make it. Why? Because all of a sudden he decides he has to *schlep* around the globe for two years."

schlock (shlock)—Junk, crap, inferior merchandise or meretricious work, e.g., "Eminem's Christmas album? *Schlock!*" Addition of *-y* yields *schlocky*, meaning crappy, lousy, cheap-o. Further variations (schlock-o, Schlock City, Schlock-o-rama) are post-Yiddish constructions, and beyond the scope of the present inquiry. Plus they're kind of *schlocky*.

schmatte (SHMAH-teh)–A rag, a cheap piece of clothing. Often used to describe a favorite old garment you just can't get rid of, no matter how decrepit. Also, according to your mother, something you are not leaving this house wearing.

schmo (shmo)–A hapless sucker, an ordinary jerk. Slightly pejorative, but it could be worse (e.g., could be *putz* or *schmuck*).

schmooze (shmooz)–To have a friendly, gossipy, heart-to-heart talk or chat. Or to cultivate socially, usually in conversation; to suck up to or kiss ass.

schnoz (schnahz)–Nose. *Schnozzola* (schnah-ZO-lah) is (archaic) American-Yiddish slang for the same thing.

shanda (SHAHN-dah)–Not only a pity or a shame, but a scandalous shame, an affront to decency. Back in the sixties, during the wild and krazee trial of the Chicago Seven, Yippie goofmeister (and defendant) Abbie Hoffman protested the proceedings by shouting at the judge, Julius Hoffman (no relation), *"Shanda far di goyim!"*

What Abbie meant was, roughly, "It is a scandal that you—a Jew, whose ethnic history of oppression should have made your moral sense more acute than most—are presiding over this outrageous, trumped-up, repressive show trial, and, in the presence of and in collusion with Gentiles! Who, let's face it, we sometimes quietly pride ourselves in setting an example for in terms of secular morality."

sheygets (SHAY-gits)–A Gentile male. (A Gentile female is a *shiksa*.) Usually used with pejorative connotations, but not in this book, because we're nice.

shlemiel (shleh-MEEL)–A foolish person, a sucker, a sap; an unlucky person; a clumsy person. The classic distinction between a *shlemiel* and a *shlimazl* is, the *shlemiel* spills his soup, and the *shlimazl* is the one he spills it on. More a term of pity than opprobrium.

shmegegge (shmeh-GEG-ee, all *g*'s being hard)– An unadmirable person, a nobody, an ordinary Joe who lacks the talent, intelligence, or moral stature to be considered a full-fledged person. Mildly pejorative. Most often used in the hypothetical/ general sense, e.g., "Then she moved to Miami and married some *shmegegge*."

shmy (shmy)–To stroll, meander, window-shop. Unlike *tanz*, which is done with attitude, *shmy* is more of an aimless walk. "They *shmyed* from one end of the mall to the other, just killing time."

shnorrers (SHNORR-erz)–Literally, "beggars." Moochers, freeloaders. Which is not to suggest a lack of discrimination. *A shnorrer* will pile up his plate with shrimp, yes, but he will not take a bunch of matchbooks (or yarmulkes) with the Bar Mitzvah boy's name on them *even though he could.*

shpilkes (SHPILL-kiss)–Pins and needles; edge, as in "on edge." Mothers "sit on *shpilkes*" until their children get back to *Hotzeplotz* and call to say they arrived safely.

shtikl (SHTICK-l)–A little bit, slightly, somewhat. "Why is she shouting? Because she's a *shtikl* deaf, that's why."

shtunk (shtoonk, where the "oo" rhymes with "hook")–A stinker, a jerk, an asshole, a nasty person. An example of Yiddish onomotopaeia, or however you spell it.

shtupping (SHTOOP-ing, where the first syllable rhymes with the singular of "whoops!")–Having sex, fornicating, etc. It can mean either doing it right this second ("Look! They're *shtupping*!") or doing it in a general, ongoing way ("'Good friends'? Don't kid yourself. They're *shtupping*").

shtuss (shtooss, where the "oo" rhymes with "hook") – In this case, a commotion, a to-do. Can also mean nonsense, poppycock, balderdash.

simcha (SIM-chuh) – A blessing. A happy, joyous occasion that merits celebration. "Talk about a *simcha* — the brisket was on sale *and* I had a coupon!"

takeh (TAH-keh) – Literally, "truly." Thus, "*I'll* say," "on stilts," "with a vengeance," "*really,*" etc. Used to amplify the emphasis of the basic assertion. "Her face doesn't move. That's *takeh* some Botox job."

tanz (tahnss) – Literally, "dance." To sweep into a room with attitude; to waltz in. "I had a standing appointment with the Eyebrow Nazi every other Saturday at 10 a.m. She would always *tanz* herself in at 10:20 as if she hadn't kept me waiting for twenty minutes."

tsedoodelt (tseh-DOOD-elt, where the middle syllable rhymes with "good") – Confused, mixed-up, wacky. While there seem to be a number of Yiddish words to describe this addled state (and in increasing levels of severity), there seems to be no word meaning, simply, happy. The reason? Jews are allowed to be publicly confused, but a public declaration of happiness invites reprisals from the Evil Eye.

tsedreyt in kop (tseh-DRAYT in KOP or KUP)– Literally, "turned around in the head." Can be used in reference to someone who is disoriented or confused, but mostly used when describing someone who doesn't take your advice.

tsimmes (TSIM-miss)–Literally, a dish of cooked vegetables (sweet potatoes, carrots) and dried fruits (prunes, raisins), usually with honey. It's complicated to prepare. Thus, figuratively, a big deal, a complicated matter, a federal case. "Look, let's not make a *tsimmes* out of it. We'll go in separate cars."

tsuris (TSOOR-iss)–Troubles, problems, woes. What constitutes *tsuris* depends on a person's tolerance level. The range can encompass everything from a leaky faucet in your kitchen to a malfunction in your space capsule. "Houston, we have *tsuris*."

tuchas (TOOCH-iss, rhymes with "book-kiss")–Rear end, behind, ass, etc. The present usage ("gets up off his *tuchas*") suggests the narrators think Bob is lazy, which we actually don't.

vo den (VUH DEN, in which both syllables are accentuated; rhymes with "good men")–"What else?" "What did you expect?" "Don't tell me you're surprised." And so on. Actually, the most concise way of describing this is to say it means "So *nu?*"

zaftig (ZAHF-tig)–Usually with regard to a woman: pleasingly plump, large-breasted, ample. Whether used as a sincere term of flattery or as a euphemism for...you know...*fat*, depends on the speaker. A slim woman with large breasts would usually not be called *zaftig*. (Like she would care.)

zetz (zets)–A hit, a punch, a blow. More forceful than a *klop*, which is a whack. A *klop in keppe* is mildly rebuking, like "a hit upside the head." A *zetz* is a real sock.

About the Authors

ELLIS WEINER has been an editor of *National Lampoon*, a columnist for *Spy*, and a contributor to many magazines, including *The New Yorker*, the *New York Times Magazine*, *Mademoiselle*, and the *Paris Review*. His recent books include a novel, *Drop Dead, My Lovely* (NAL, March 2004), and *The Joy of Worry*, with illustrations by Roz Chast (Chronicle, June 2004). He lives in Bethlehem, Pennsylvania.

BARBARA DAVILMAN began her career in New York in advertising, created and ran her own greeting card company (which was featured in *People* magazine and on the *Today* show), and was then summoned to Los Angeles to write for sitcoms that, thankfully, no one remembers.

GABI PAYN, illustrator of *Yiddish with Dick and Jane*, has worked in television animation for many years and lives in Los Angeles.